WO'I BWIKAM
COYOTE SONGS

WO'I BWIKAM
COYOTE SONGS

from the Yaqui Bow Leaders' Society

recorded, translated, and annotated by

Larry Evers & Felipe S. Molina

Chax Press

Tucson, Arizona 1990

Felipe thanks all the boys who participate in the Bow Leaders' Society at Yoem Pueblo, especially Victor Lucero. He also thanks Raul Cancio for his efforts to form the group and Jenny Cancio for feeding the group during practice sessions. *Lios em chiokoe utteasia.*

Other versions of this essay appeared in Laura Coltelli, ed., *Native American Literatures* (Pisa, Italy: University of Pisa, 1988) and, with an introduction by Karl Kroeber, in *Dispatch* (Fall, 1988), a publication of the Columbia University Center for American Culture Studies.

Chax Press wishes to thank the DeGrazia Arts and Cultural Foundation, Inc., and the Foundation Cariñoso, without whom this publication would not have been possible. Additional funding in support of this book has come from the Arizona Commission on the Arts and the National Endowment for the Arts.

A handprinted, deluxe edition of this book, in 100 copies, is being published simultaneously with this edition. Special thanks go to Cynthia Miller for her illustrations for both editions.

This book is printed and bound in the United States of America.

Library of Congress Cataloging-in-Publication Data

Coyote songs = Wo'i bwikam : songs from the Yaqui Bow Leaders' Society / recorded, translated, and annotated by Larry Evers and Felipe S. Molina.
    p.   cm.
  English and Yaqui.
  Bibliography: p.
  $200.00 (deluxe pbk.). — $8.00
    1. Yaqui poetry.   2. Yaqui Indians — Rites and ceremonies.
  3. Indians of North America — Arizona — Rites and ceremonies.
  4. Indians of Mexico — Mexico — Sonora (State) — Rites and ceremonies.
  5. Yaqui poetry — Translations into English.   6. America poetry — Translations from Yaqui.
  I. Evers, Larry.   II. Molina, Felipe S.   III. Yaqui Bow Leaders' Society.
  IV. Title: Wo'i bwikam.
  PM4526.Z77C6   1990
  897'.4 — dc19   89-680
  ISBN 0-925904-01-5 (handprinted, deluxe)
  ISBN 0-925904-02-3 (trade paperback)

Chax Press is located at 101 West Sixth Street, no. 4, Tucson, Arizona 85701.

Part 1

How the Coyotes Came Back to Old Pascua

contexts

April 11, 1987, on the eve of Palm Sunday,
with an Easter moon on the rise, the Coyotes came back to Old Pascua. And with them came a traditional genre of poetic expression that has not been performed in that Yaqui Indian community since 1941.

We write to tell a part of the story of that return and to offer transcriptions and translations of the nine songs to which the Coyotes danced the night they came back.

Victor Lucero, Timothy Cruz, Steven Garcia, Felipe Garcia, and Joaquin Garcia were the Coyotes who danced that night. Felipe S. Molina sang for them. Their performance was the culmination of a long period of preparation. Felipe Molina remembers the events that led to that performance this way:

About 1982 Larry Evers gave me a copy of some Coyote songs that Amos Taub had collected from Yaqui elders, such as Ignacio Alvarez and Refugio Savala, in the Tucson area in the early 1950s. This collection provided me with new songs that I could learn to sing. I went ahead and practiced the songs for my own interest, but as I practiced I was keeping in mind that maybe one day I would sing for some Bow Leader dancers.

It so happens that in my village the young boys, ranging in ages from, let's say, six to about eighteen, are interested in doing various forms of Yaqui dance and song. Some of the boys have learned many deer songs. They all have performed in a village or household pahko. *Some have also learned some of the steps and movements of the deer dance. Because I have been working with these boys, I have been noticed in the Yaqui communities around Tucson. That is how Raul Cancio came into the picture.*

For many months Raul Cancio tried to get in touch with me to talk about the Bow Leaders. I always forgot to call him back or to leave a message for him. Victor Lucero is one of the boys that I sing with in the village. Victor pushed me along the way to get a Bow Leader group formed. He was the person that kept telling me that Raul Cancio wanted to talk to me about forming a Bow Leaders group. I didn't give much thought to the idea then, but it always stayed somewhere in my mind.

So finally in the fall of 1985 I met Raul Cancio for the first time, and we talked awhile about ourselves. He knew something about me, but he was a complete stranger to me. However, I knew his wife because she was a god-mother to my nephew. Anyway, from this conversation developed the notion that we would start a Bow Leader group and that Raul would provide the necessary headdresses and other regalia if I would sing. We decided to hold the practice sessions in Yoem Pueblo at my house. So through this meeting our friendship was made and a Bow Leaders group was formed at Yoem Pueblo.

I did not intend to be in Old Pascua at all during the Holy Week ceremonials in 1987. I had intended to go to Potam in the Rio Yaqui area, so that I could see the Looria there. But I was given a god-child to sponsor for Holy Saturday in Old Pascua, so I could not go. So with that responsibility I had to stay for Holy Saturday. Since I was going to be there I was asked to sing for the deer dancer during the Palm Sunday pahko *and also again to sing for him during the Looria and the Holy Saturday* pahko.

Before Lent, Victor Lucero kept asking me if the new Bow Leaders group could participate in the Easter ceremonies. I said I didn't really know because I thought I might go to Potam. So we never got started at the beginning of Lent. So finally Palm Saturday was approaching so Victor got on my case again and wanted to know if the group could dance at the pahko. *I told him that I really couldn't tell him yes or no because I was going to be singing for the deer dancer. He said I could alternate between the Bow Leaders and the Deer. Finally through much contemplation I agreed and told him I would talk to the Fariseo Captain. The Captain was delighted to hear the request. He said* heewi, *it would be wonderful. So it seems that the group, especially Victor, was very happy to participate in the ceremonials. The group all went and danced and participated in the* pahko. *I alternated between the two groups all night long, first singing the Deer Songs inside the* rama *with the raspers, then going outside with the drum to sing Coyote Songs. Yaqui people were very happy to see and hear the two groups. All the non-Yaquis who came seemed very happy, too, but most of them did not know what we were doing. They thought that the Bow Leaders were part of the deer dance.*

I am grateful to Victor for his determination. He convinced me to accept his suggestion.

Wo'im, Coyotes, is what most Yaquis call them now. But in the talk of Yaqui elders they are appropriately called *Wiko'i Yau'ura*, the Bow Leaders. The Bow Leaders have served Yaqui communities for centuries as a military society. They are mentioned in the writing of a Jesuit missionary who worked among the Yaquis in the 1730s. Two and one-half centuries later, the Bow Leaders remain active in many of the towns along the Rio Yaqui on the wide coastal plain south of Guaymas, Sonora: Torim, Vikam, Potam, Rahum, Pitahaya, Loma Vahkom.

As recently as 1927, the Coyotes took up their bows and arrows and their rifles against Mexicans who were attempting yet again to appropriate Yaqui lands. Today they are most visible during certain *pahkom*, ceremonial occasions when Yaquis gather to perform religious rituals and to celebrate. On these occasions the Coyotes dance and perform burlesques to special songs, as they work to entertain those drawn to their performances. What they do with their songs and their dances is playful, light-hearted, fun. But their dance and song contribute, too, to their most fundamental role and their most serious duty: the Bow Leaders are the stewards of *Hiakim*, the Yaqui homeland, and they are bound by sacred vows to protect it.

The main function of a Bow Leader was to protect the land for the people. Nowadays the society's main function is a religious duty. The Bow Leaders have many obligations to the church and other ceremonial activities throughout the year. At the same time they act like guardians during a ceremonial to keep drinking and fighting out of the plaza or the household patio where a ceremonial is taking place.

Before the person decides to become a lifetime member he or she goes through many hours of counsel to get a better view of how it is to be a member. Many sad stories are told about how hard it can be during certain ceremonies when there is no food, when the weather is too cold or too hot, or when fatigue makes carrying out the duty very difficult. Stories are told that death is probable in times of war and that the one who is initiated could become food for the wild animals or the vultures.

The modern initiation ritual takes place in the church. The person who wants to be initiated formally tells the officials of the Bow Leaders. After hearing the speech the officials accept the person and answer in a formal speech. During this time the date for the initiation ritual is set so that both parties are satisfied with the date. Then it is up to the joining person to look for a god-father and a god-mother to help. The god-parents are usually members in the Bow Leaders, but not always. They can be Bow Leaders from a different village.

The initiation ceremony is carried out in the church around mid-morning. Starting at the church altar the god-parents are on either side of their god-child, the man on the right and the woman on the left. They walk out together to the elder cross in the plaza. They walk from the altar to the elder cross three times going in a counter clockwise direction. The new member is dressed completely in the Bow Leader regalia, including his bow and a quiver with several arrows. After the third trip they stop in front of the church altar and the new member kneels down.

The initiation involves being blessed with a Yaqui rosary and then with a small crucifix. Finally the new member will be pushed down to the floor three times. This concludes the church part of the ritual. Back at the Bow Leaders Headquarters a formal reception speech is given and a feast takes place. There is dancing at intervals. Both the Bow Leaders members and those spectators who are formally requested can dance. However, the first three songs are danced by the captain of the Bow Leaders and two soldiers. After that visitors will be invited to dance. This celebration will continue into the early evening.

Our Bow Leaders group in Yoem Pueblo is still only a few years old and none of the members here in Arizona have gone through a formal initiation. I do not know if they will.

The presence of the Bow Leaders Society in Arizona has always been tenuous. Members of the group probably first came to live in Arizona with other Yaqui refugees who were forced out of their homeland in southern Sonora in the 1890s and early 1900s. During those years around the turn of the century Yaquis suffered brutal oppression from a Mexican government bent on deportation and outright genocide as ways of possessing the rich well-watered farmland of the Yaquis. Thousands of Yaquis were captured and sent to work as slaves in Yucatan. Other Yaquis managed to escape north over the border into southern Arizona. These Yaquis brought many of their cultural traditions with them to this place that some older Yaquis still call "Ringo Bwia," Gringo Land.

During the 1920s a Bow Leaders group formed at the village we now call Old Pascua in Tucson, and they continued to perform through the 1930s. The last remembered performance was in 1941. Edward H. Spicer suggests that because the Bow Leader Society was so tied to *Hiakim*, the Yaqui homeland, it "had no immediate significance for Yaquis who had decided to forsake the tribal territory and make their home indefinitely in new and different land."

It may be significant then that recent revival of the Coyote society in southern Arizona follows the acquisition of community lands here. In the 1960s a group of Yaquis acquired title to some 202 acres from the federal government and moved there to establish the community known as New Pascua. That community has now grown to about a thousand acres of land. In 1980 Yaquis living in Yoem Pueblo were able to purchase the land upon which their village rests from the private water company that owned it. These small parts of *Ringo Bwia* are not now and, likely, will never be regarded as *Hiakim* by Yaquis. But over the more than eighty years they have lived in southern Arizona Yaquis have named and imagined the landscape around their communities in ways that echo their homeland. The revival of the Coyote society may be a sign that they are ready to take a role as stewards of the space they have been imagining.

The first time I heard about the Coyotes was when I was growing up in my grandparents' house. My grandparents didn't talk too much about them but I remember that they said that they should be called the Bow Leaders.

What first interested me about the Bow Leaders was the time in 1971 when they were supposed to appear at New Pascua. People were excited to hear that a Bow Leaders group was coming from the Yaqui country in Sonora to participate in the Christo Rey pahko. *The night of the* pahko, *at that particular time when the Bow Leaders were supposed to dance, the plaza at New Pascua was packed.*

But what was disappointing was that the Bow Leaders did not dance. They just sat there. Finally about 1:00 or 2:00 AM they began to dance. A big circle formed around the area where the group danced. What fascinated me was the headdress. I enjoyed watching the way the hawk feathers flew as the Coyotes danced. The dancers were not very enthusiastic and the singing was hard to hear. So I was not impressed by this group. But what happened in the early morning hours as we drove to our home near Marana did impress me. A coyote ran across the road in front of us. Everybody yelled, "Look, Wo'i!"

Yaquis think of the natural world of the Sonoran Desert as one living community. This community is called *huya ania*, the wilderness world. One of the things that binds those who live in the *huya ania* together is a common language, the language of song. Like deer songs, coyote songs are a part of this language of the wilderness world. They may describe or give a voice to any of the inhabitants of the *huya ania*: coyote, rattlesnake, skunk, badger, fox, dragonfly, crow, vultures, the desert tortoise, to name a few. Others that may be referred to in the songs are *sewa yoleme* (flower person), *yo yoleme* (enchanted person), and *machiwa yoleme* (dawn person). *Yoeme* is the Yaqui word for person. *Yoemem*, People, is what Yaquis call themselves in their own language. The *yoemem* who appear in the songs—the flower person, the enchanted person, the dawn person—are persons who have special relationships with the other inhabitants of the wilderness world. Coyote songs may also describe the dancers and the objects with which they dance: their headdresses, their bows and arrows. There are songs, too, that are mostly about Christian figures such as Saint Francis, Saint Peter, Saint Paul, Saint John and so on. Felipe considers these songs about the saints to be newer songs.

Like deer songs, the songs of the Bow Leaders have two parts: *u vat weeme*, the first part, which is repeated three or four times or more, and *u tonua*, the concluding part, which is sung once to complete the song. We give only one repetition of the first part for the songs that we transcribe and translate here.

The dancers' movements are keyed to these two parts of the song: the first part is sung over and over as the dancers dance away from the singer, the concluding part as they dance back to the place in front of him where they began. The singer uses a different drum rhythm for each of the two parts. Because of this, it is said that during the concluding part "the drum calls them back," *u kuvahe ameu chai*.

The singer may choose to sing any of the coyote songs that he knows. In that sense, there is no fixed sequence of songs. However, a song called *Sontao Ya'uchim*, Soldier Leaders, is usually the first song sung, and, like deer songs, the other songs follow a progression through evening songs, midnight songs and morning songs. The subjects of the songs and the manner in which they are danced gets increasingly playful as the night progresses. The songs that we translate here are given in the order in which Felipe sang them at Old Pascua.

The singer accompanies himself with a drum. There is a sounding hole in the rim of the drum, and traditionally the singer sings directly into that hole. It can be difficult, then, to hear exactly what he is saying. This is a performance tradition that singers take advantage of or not depending on the occasion.

BIBLIOGRAPHICAL NOTE

Yaqui Deer Songs/Maso Bwikam: A Native American Poetry (Tucson: Sun Tracks and the University of Arizona Press, 1987) tells how we understand our collaboration and the work of translating Yaqui verbal arts for non-Yaqui audiences. In that book, we review earlier attempts to record and translate Yaqui verbal arts, as well as approaches to the translation, interpretation, and appreciation of the verbal arts throughout native America.

Edward H. Spicer's *The Yaquis: A Cultural History* (Tucson: University of Arizona Press, 1980) provides a comprehensive discussion of Yaqui history and culture. See especially pages 164–176 for his discussion of the Coyote Society as protectors of Yaqui lands. Muriel Thayer Painter, *With Good Heart: Yaqui Beliefs and Ceremonies in Pascua Village* (Tucson: University of Arizona Press, 1986), is an encyclopedic work made from the direct testimony of dozens of anonymous Yaqui consultants. We have quoted Refugio Savala, a.k.a. informant "55," from this work. See Felipe S. Molina and Larry Evers, "Muriel Thayer Painter's *With Good Heart*: Two Views," *Journal of the Southwest*, 29, No. 1 (Spring 1987), pp. 96–106.

Ruth Warner Giddings gathered the only substantive collection of Yaqui narratives as an M.A. thesis under Professor Edward Spicer's direction in 1945. We quote from that work, "Folk Literature of the Yaqui Indians," rather than the version of it that was published as *Yaqui Myths and Legends* (Tucson: University of Arizona Press, 1959). Leticia Varela, an ethnomusicologist at the University of Hermosillo, includes commentary on the Coyote Society in her study *La Musica en La Vida de Los Yaquis* (Hermosillo, Sonora: Secretaria de Fomento Educativo y Cultura, 1986). Of particular interest is her transcription of a formal speech made for initiates to the Bow Leader Society. See pages 50–55.

Amos Taub prepared "Traditional Poetry of the Yaqui Indians," an M.A. thesis (University of Arizona, 1950), under the direction of Edward Spicer and Frances Gillmor.

Part 2

What They Sang

songs

eme sontao ya'uchim
vanseka
tu'ulisi
chomoka
hisaka

yewi yewima
katema
yewi yewima
katema

katema
katema
katema
katema

vanseka
tu'ulisi
tavelo masata
sialapti
chomoka
hisaka

yewi yewima
katema
yewi yewima
katema

katema
katema
katema
katema
katema

This song describes the dancers the first time they are coming out at a ceremony.

You soldier leaders
　　go ahead
　　　　beautifully
　　　　　　with the mask
　　　　　　　　with the headdress

Out out
　　then walk
　　　　out out
　　　　　　then walk

Walk
　　walk
　　　　walk
　　　　　　walk

Go ahead
　　beautifully
　　　　with a parrot wing
　　　　　　covered green
　　　　　　　　with the mask
　　　　　　　　　　with the headdress

Out out
　　then walk
　　　　out out
　　　　　　then walk

Walk
　　walk
　　　　walk
　　　　　　walk
　　　　　　　　walk

The first time the bow dancers come out they bless the ground in the four directions: first to the east then the north, the south, and finally the west. This is called *kusaroapo bwiata teochiawame*, blessing the earth in the way of the cross. The bow dancers do this because they have a special obligation to protect *Hiakim*, the sacred lands of the Yaquis.

yoyo vaka hiuwa
   yoyo vaka hiuwa

hakunsa vo'oka
   masa moye
      masa moye

yoyo vaka hiuwa
   yoyo vaka hiuwa

hakunsa vo'oka
   masa moye
      masa moye

masa moye
   moye
      moye
         moye
            moye

ayamansu seyewailo saniloapo huyapo
   hikatsu vo'oka
      masa moye
         masa moye

yoyo vaka hiuwa
   yoyo vaka hiuwa

hakunsa vo'oka
   masa moye
      masa masa moye

masa moye
   moye
      moye
         moye
            moye

Masa, wing, refers to the feathers used as fletching; *vaka*, bamboo, to a local bamboo called *carrizo* in Spanish. *Carrizo* is used for many functions in Yaqui country: the walls of traditional houses are *carrizo*, canes are split and woven to create baskets and floor mats, flutes are crafted from *carrizo*, and, as this song suggests, so are arrows.

Enchanted enchanted bamboo arrow
  enchanted enchanted bamboo arrow

Where are you lying?
  with wing decaying
    with wing decaying

Enchanted enchanted bamboo arrow
  enchanted enchanted bamboo arrow

Where are you lying?
  with wing decaying
    with wing decaying

Wing decaying
  decaying
    decaying
      decaying
        decaying

Over there in the flower-covered mesquite grove
  on a tree top you are lying
    with wing decaying
      with wing decaying

Enchanted enchanted bamboo arrow
  enchanted enchanted bamboo arrow

Where are you lying?
  with wing decaying
    with wing decaying

Wing decaying
  decaying
    decaying
      decaying
        decaying

Refugio Savala recalled a story about a Yaqui woman, Ana Maria, who took a giant Yaqui bowman out to *Takalaim*, the mountain with the forked peaks that rises above San Carlos Bay, north of Guaymas, Sonora. From *Takalaim* the bowman shot his bow four times to define the boundary of the Yaqui lands. There is a story about another Yaqui bowman who had a contest with the King of Spain during the time of the Conquest. Both shot arrows in the four directions from the center of Yaqui lands. Because the Yaqui shot his arrows farther, the King of Spain gave Yaquis a written title to their land.

yoyo vaikumarewi
    yo va'ata vepasu
        cha'aka
            masata yowa

yoyo vaikumarewi
    yo va'ata vepasu
        cha'aka
            haivusu masata yowa

masata yowa
    yowa
        yowa
            yowa

ayamansu seyewailo
    yo va'ata
        maneka vepa
            cha'aka
                haivusu masata yowa

yoyo vaikumarewi
    yo va'ata vepasu
        cha'aka
            haivusu masata yowa

masata yowa
    yowa
        yowa
            yowa
                yowa

Enchanted enchanted dragonfly
  above the enchanted water
    is hovering
      wing shaking

Enchanted enchanted dragonfly
  above the enchanted water
    is hovering
      wing already shaking

Wing shaking
  shaking
    shaking
      shaking

Over there above the flower-covered
  enchanted water
    where it sits
      it is hovering
        wing already shaking

Enchanted enchanted dragonfly
  above the enchanted water
    is hovering
      wing already shaking

Wing shaking
  shaking
    shaking
      shaking
        shaking

kooni
    hitasa mahaika
        saiyula vo'oka
           saiyula vo'oka

kooni kooni
    hitasa mahaika
        saiyula vo'oka
           saiyula vo'oka

vo'oka
    vo'oka
        vo'oka
           vo'oka

katikun
    vaka hiuwata mahaika
    wamsu
        saiyula vo'oka

saiyula vo'oka

    kooni kooni
        hitasa mahaika
           saiyula vo'oka
              saiyula vo'oka

vo'oka
    vo'oka
        vo'oka
           vo'oka

Crow
　　what are you afraid of?
　　　　huddled lying
　　　　　　huddled lying

Crow crow
　　what are you afraid of?
　　　　huddled lying
　　　　　　huddled lying

Lying
　　lying
　　　　lying
　　　　　　lying

Don't you remember
　　you are afraid of
　　　　the bamboo arrow over there?
　　　　　　huddled lying

Huddled lying

Crow crow
　　what are you afraid of?
　　　　huddled lying
　　　　　　huddled lying

Lying
　　lying
　　　　lying
　　　　　　lying

San Juan
    San Pasihkota wiko'i
        su kottak

San Juan
    San Pasihkota wiko'i
        su kottak

kottak
    kottak
        kottak
            kottak

machiauvicha
    su kitteka
        haitowikti a
            wikeka
                kottak

machiauvicha
    su kitteka
        haitowikti a
            wikeka
                kottak

kottak
    kottak
        kottak
        kottak

In the early 1940s, Lucas Chavez, a singer from Old Pascua, told folklorist Ruth Warner Giddings:

Coyote dancers . . . attend the annual celebrations to San Francis at Magdelena, Sonora . . . they worship the Saint by dancing to a song which praises Saint Francis as a great Yaqui soldier who was able to kill a very powerful bird called *kupahe*. The feathers of this bird are worn in the coyote dancers' headdress.

Saint John
the bow of Saint Francis
did break

Saint John
the bow of Saint Francis
did break

Break
break
break
break

Toward the dawn
he did stand
snapped
pulled
broke it

Toward the dawn
he did stand
snapped
pulled
broke it

Break
break
break
break

About the same time Refugio Savala told Muriel Thayer Painter:

Another old song refers to San Francisco Xavier being in the army as a soldier. San Pedro is supposed to have borrowed a bow and arrow from San Francisco Xavier and to have pulled on the bow until it broke.

San Peo
  teeka pwetapo kateka
    tu'uwata noka

San Peo
  teeka pwetapo kateka
    tu'uwata noka

noka
  noka
    noka
      noka

ayamansu
  seyewailo santo
    teweka looria pwetapo katek
      tu'uwata noka

San Peo
  teeka pwetapo kateka
    tu'uwata noka

noka
  noka
    noka
      noka

Refugio Savala, again to Muriel Thayer Painter in the 1940s:

[Saint Peter] is supposed to be the captain of the army, and the advisor of the army. He is in a coyote song for dancing, and, in a way, it says that San Pedro sits at the gate of headquarters and advises the soldiers.

Saint Peter
    sitting at heaven's door
        goodness talks

Saint Peter
    sitting at heaven's door
        goodness talks

Talks
    talks
        talks
            talks

Over there
    sitting at the flower-covered
        holy heaven's door
            goodness talks

Saint Peter
    sitting at heaven's door
        goodness talks

Talks
    talks
        talks
            talks

eme sontao ya'uchim
tulisi hepela
kateka
nausu yewe
nausu yewe

eme sontao ya'uchim
tulisi hepela
kateka
nausu yewe
nausu yewe

yewe
yewe
yewe
yewe

imsu sewa votsu
hepela kateka
nausu yewe

eme sontao ya'uchim
tulisi hepela
kateka
nausu yewe
nausu yewe

yewe
yewe
yewe
yewe

The Bow Leaders dance three at a time. Their usual formation is not *natchaka kaate,* one after the other walking, nor *mochala,* bunched up as in a crowd, but rather, as this song describes them, *hepela,* side by side.

You soldier leaders
    beautifully side by side
        are walking
            together playing
                together playing

You soldier leaders
    beautifully side by side
        are walking
            together playing
                together playing

Playing
    playing
        playing
            playing

Here on the flower road
    side by side you are walking
        together playing

You soldier leaders
    beautifully side by side
        are walking
            together playing
                together playing

Playing
    playing
        playing
            playing

Side by side, in rhythm and perfectly in step is the definitive posture of their dance. But like the deer dancer and the *pahkolam* they may perform *yeuwame*, plays, in which they act out certain songs. In one, often performed near the end of the *pahko*, the people who are giving the *pahko* put out a plate of barbecued meat on the ground between the singer and the dancers. The singer sings about coyotes as the dancers dance out in their usual way, then turn around and dance in backwards, dropping to all fours only at the last instant and fighting like coyotes over the plate of meat. Then they resume dancing in their usual position, *hepela*, side by side, but now one coyote has meat in his mouth.

yoyo a'akame
    sevipo vo'oka

siirisiiriti hia
    siirisiiriti hia
        siirisiiriti hia

hia
    hia
        hia
            hia

katikun
    taewalita sumeiyaka
        haivusu sevipo vo'oka

siirisiiriti hia
    siirisiiriti hia
        siirisiiriti hia

hia
    hia
        hia
            hia

The word for rattles is *ayam*.

Enchanted enchanted rattlesnake
 in the cactus is lying

Siirisiiri sounding
 siirisiiri sounding
  siirisiiri sounding

Sounding
 sounding
  sounding
   sounding

Remember
 he is frightened of the day
  already in the cactus lying

Siirisiiri sounding
 siirisiiri sounding
  siirisiiri sounding

Sounding
 sounding
  sounding
   sounding

This is a play song. When Felipe sings it, the dancers dance all the way out during the repetitions of the first stanza as usual but when the concluding stanza begins, "when the drum calls them back," they get down on the ground and slither like snakes.

hupa
    hu'upa kutapo
        kateka

to'e to'eti hia
    to'e to'eti hia
        to'e to'eti hia

hia
    hia
        hia
            hia

katikun
    yo hu'upapo
        kateka
            to'e to'eti hia
                to'e to'eti hia

hupa
    hu'upa kutapo
        kateka

to'e to'eti hia
    to'e to'eti hia
        to'e to'eti hia

hia
    hia
        hia
            hia

Some older Yaquis use a tongue twister that plays with sounds like this song. The tongue twister goes like this:

hupa hu'upapo	skunk in mesquite
vetuku kateka	under sitting
huvam huhak	stinky farted